Campfire Songs

D1563726

CAMPFIRE SONGS

Lyrics and Chords to
More Than 100 Sing-Along Favorites

FOURTH EDITION

EDITED BY
Irene Maddox and Rosalyn Cobb

FALCON GUIDES

GUILFORD, CONNECTICUT
HELENA, MONTANA
AN IMPRINT OF GLOBE PEQUOT PRESS

*To my husband, Robert, with many thanks for all his help
and support with this book.*
—IRENE MADDOX

To all my students, who continue to teach me so much about life.
—ROSALYN COBB

To buy books in quantity for corporate use
or incentives, call **(800) 962–0973**
or e-mail **premiums@GlobePequot.com.**

Music set by Darryl Gregory/Blue Cave Studios

Text design: Sheryl Kober
Project editor: Julie Marsh
Layout: Lisa Nanamaker

ISBN 978-0-7627-6387-0

Printed in the United States of America

10 9 8 7 6 5 4 3 2 1

Contents

AMERICAN FOLK SONGS

Contents

Introduction

Singing around a campfire or fireplace has been a natural and enjoyable way to close a day of hiking, camping, or work for centuries. Since recorded history began, we know that singing has been a major entertainment for many people.

Many songs have been passed down from one generation to another. Melodies have been altered to fit the singer or the place, but the spirit of the music lives on, giving us songs to cheer us when we are down, inspire us when we are tired, and soothe us when we are troubled.

Breaking into song wherever we are—in the car, in the shower, at work, or at play—is second nature to us. The songs we sing are usually the ones we remember from our parents or from our childhood songfests around a campfire.

It is the editors' hope that the songs in this collection will rekindle fond memories of good times, and that these strong memories will become an integral part of keeping our folk song heritage alive.

Songs of the West (Cowboy)

Get Along Little Dogies

(WHOOPEE TI-YI-YO/DOGIE SONG)

1. As I was a walking one mor - ning for pleasure, I
spied a cow - pun - cher a rid - ing a - long. His
hat was thrown back and his spurs were a jing - ling, And
as he ap - proached he was sing - ing this song:

Chorus

Whoo - pee ti - yi - yo, ___ get a - long lit - tle dog - ies, It's
your mis - for - tune and none of my own.

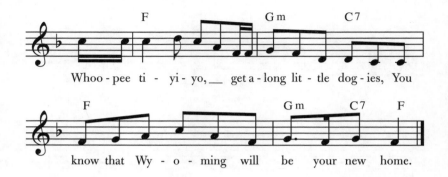

Whoo - pee ti - yi - yo, __ get a - long lit - tle dog - ies, You
know that Wy - o - ming will be your new home.

2. It's early in spring when we round up the dogies,
   And mark them and brand them and bob off their tails,
   We round up our horses and load the chuck wagon,
   And then herd the dogies right out on the trail. (*Chorus*)

Goodbye, Old Paint

1. My foot in the stir - rup, my po - ny won't stan'; ___ I'm leav - ing Chey - enne and I'm off to Mon - tan'. ___

Chorus Good - bye, old Paint I'm a - leav - ing Chey - enne.

2. I'm riding old Paint and I'm leading old Fan;
   Goodbye little Annie, I'm off for Montan'. (*Chorus*)

3. Oh, keep yourself by me as long as you can;
   Goodbye little Annie, I'm off for Montan'. (*Chorus*)

Home on the Range

1. Oh, give me a home where the buf - fa - lo roam, Where the deer and the an - te - lope play; _____ Where sel - dom is heard a dis - cour - a-ging word, And the sky is not clou - dy all day. _____

Chorus

Home, home on the range, _____ where the deer and the an - te - lope

play; _____ Where sel - dom is heard a dis -

cour - a-ging word, And the sky is not clou-dy all day. _____

2. How often at night when the heavens are bright
   From the light of the glittering stars
   Have I stood there, amazed, and asked as I gazed
   If their glory exceeds that of ours. (*Chorus*)

3. Where the air is so pure and the zephyrs so free,
   And the breezes so balmy and light,
   Oh, I would not exchange my home on the range
   For the glittering cities so bright. (*Chorus*)

4. Oh, give me the land where the bright diamond sand
   Flows leisurely down with the stream,
   Where the graceful, white swan glides slowly along
   Like a maid in a heavenly dream. (*Chorus*)

I Ride an Old Paint

1. I ride an old Paint,_____ I lead an old Dan,___ I'm goin' to Mon - ta - na to throw the hoo - li - an. They feed in the cou - lees, they wa - ter in the draw, their tails are all mat - ted, their backs are all raw.

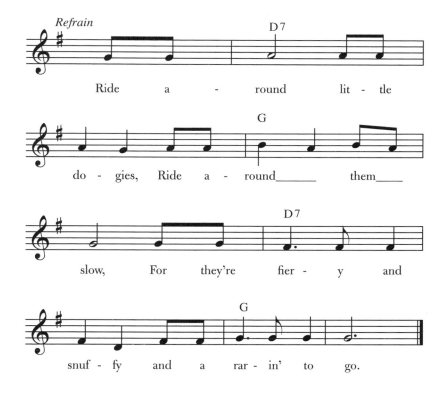

Refrain

D7

Ride a - round lit - tle

G

do - gies, Ride a - round_____ them____

D7

slow, For they're fier - y and

G

snuf - fy and a rar - in' to go.

2. Oh, when I die, take my saddle from the wall,
   And put it on my pony, lead him out of his stall.
   Tie my bones to his back, turn our faces to the west,
   And we'll ride the prairie that we love the best.
   (Refrain)

Red River Valley

1. From this val - ley they say you are go - ing, _____ we will

miss your bright eyes and sweet smile, For they say you are tak-ing the

sun - shine__ that bright - ens our path - way a - while. Come and

sit by my side if you love me, _____ Do not

has - ten to bid me a - dieu, But re - mem - ber the Red Ri -ver

Val-ley, _____ And the girl that has loved you so true.

2. Won't you think of the valley you're leaving?
   Oh, how lonely and sad it will be;
   Oh, think of the fond heart you are breaking
   And the grief you are causing to me.
   (*Refrain*)

3. I have promised you, darling, that never
   Will a word from my lips cause you pain,
   And my life, it shall be yours forever
   If you only will be mine again.
   (*Refrain*)

4. As you go to your home by the ocean,
   May you never forget those sweet hours
   That we spent in the Red River Valley
   And the love that was ours 'mid the flowers.
   (*Refrain*)

Streets of Laredo

(Cowboy's Lament)

1. As I_____ walked out in the streets of La - re - do, As I _____ walked out in La - re - do one day, I spied a young cow - boy all wrapped in white lin - en, All wrapped in white lin - en as cold as the clay.

2. "I see by your outfit that you are a cowboy,"
   These words he did say as I boldly stepped by;
   "Come, sit down beside me and hear my sad story,
   I'm shot in the breast and I'm going to die."

3. "Now once in the saddle I used to go dashing,
   Yes, once in the saddle I used to be gay,
   I'd dress myself up and go down to the card-house,
   I got myself shot and I'm dying today."

4. "Get six husky cowboys to carry my coffin,
   Get ten lovely maidens to sing me a song,
   And beat the drum slowly and play the fife lowly,
   For I'm a young cowboy who knows he was wrong."

5. "Oh, please go and bring me a cup of cold water
   To cool my parched lips they are burning," he said,
   Before I could get it, his soul had departed
   And gone to its Maker, the cowboy was dead.

6. We beat the drum slowly and played the fife lowly
   And wept in our grief as we bore him along.
   For we loved the cowboy, so brave and so handsome,
   We loved that young cowboy although he'd done wrong.

Sweet Betsy from Pike

1. Did you ev - er hear of sweet Bet - sy from Pike, Who crossed the wide prai - ries with her hus - band Ike, With two yoke of ox - en, a big yel - low dog, A___ tall Shanghai roos - ter, and one spot - ted hog, Singing *too ra li oo ra li oo ra li ay?*

2. The alkali desert was burning and bare,
   And Ike cried in fear, "We are lost, I declare!
   My dear old Pike Country, I'll come back to you!"
   Vowed Betsy, "You'll go by yourself if you do."
   Singing *too ra li oo ra li oo ra li ay.*

3. 'Twas out on the desert that Betsy gave out,
   And down in the sand she lay rolling about,
   Poor Ike, half distracted, looked down in surprise,
   Saying "Betsy, get up, you'll get sand in your eyes."
   Singing *too ra li oo ra li oo ra li ay.*

4. Then Betsy got up and gazed out on the plain,
   And said she'd go back to Pike Country again,
   But Ike heaved a sigh, and they fondly embraced,
   And they headed on west with his arm 'round her waist.
   Singing *too ra li oo ra li oo ra li ay.*

Spirituals and Gospel Hymns

All My Trials

1. Hush, lit-tle ba - by, don't you cry
You know your Ma-ma was born to
die_____ All_____ my
tri-als, Lord,_____ soon be
o - ver_____ *To Verse 2.* *Refrain** Too late, my
bro - thers,_____ Too late but ne-ver
mind,_____ All_____ my

*After 3rd and 5th verses only.

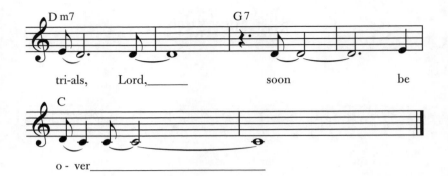

tri-als,   Lord,_____   soon   be

o - ver_____

2. The river of Jordan is muddy and cold,
   Well, it chills the body, but not the soul,
   (All my trials, Lord, soon be over.)

3. I've got a little book with pages three,
   And ev'ry page spells liberty,
   (All my trials, Lord, soon be over.)

   Too late, my brothers,
   Too late, but never mind,
   (All my trials, Lord, soon be over.)

4. If living were a thing that money could buy,
   You know the rich would live, and the poor would die,
   (All my trials, Lord, soon be over.)

5. There grows a tree in Paradise,
   And the Pilgrims call it the tree of life,
   (All my trials, Lord, soon be over.)

   Too late, my brothers,
   Too late, but never mind,
   (All my trials, Lord, soon be over.)

All Night, All Day

Amazing Grace

1. A - maz - ing ___ Grace, how sweet the sound, That ___ saved a ___ wretch like ___ me. ___ I ___ once was ___ lost, but ___ now I'm found, Was ___ blind, but ___ now I see. ___

2. Twas ___ grace that ___ taught my heart to fear, And ___ grace my ___ fear re - lieved. ___ How ___ prec - ious ___ did that ___ grace ap - pear, The ___ hour I ___ first be - lieved. ___

3. When ___ we've been ___ there ten thou - sand years, Bright ___ shi - ning ___ as the ___ sun, ___ We've ___ no less ___ days to ___ sing God's praise, Than ___ when we've ___ first be - gun. ___

(Repeat verse 1)

Spirituals and Gospel Hymns

Down by the Riverside

1. Gonna lay down my sword and shield Down by the riv - er - side, Down by the riv - er - side, Down by the riv - er - side, Gon-na lay down my sword and shield down by the riv - er - side, And stud - y_____ war no more. *Chorus* I ain't gon-na stu-dy___ war no

more, I ain't gon - na stu - dy____ war no

more, I ain't gon - na stu - dy_____ war no

1. more_____ I ain't gon - na more._____

2. I'm gonna put on my long white robe, etc.
   (*Chorus*)

3. I'm gonna talk with the Prince of Peace, etc.
   (*Chorus*)

4. I'm gonna join hands with ev'ryone, etc.
   (*Chorus*)

Spirituals and Gospel Hymns

Down in My Heart

I've got that joy, joy, joy, joy
down in my heart, down in my heart,
down in my heart. I've got that joy, joy, joy, joy
down in my heart, down in my heart to - day.

2. I've got that love of Jesus, love of Jesus,
   down in my heart, etc.

3. I've got that peace that passeth understanding
   down in my heart, etc.

Ezekiel Saw the Wheel

Get on Board

Chorus

Get on board, lit-tle chil-dren, Get on board, lit-tle chil-dren, Get on board, lit-tle chil-dren, There's room for man-y a more. 1. The

Verse

1. The gos-pel train's a com-ing, I hear it just at hand, I hear the car wheels rum-bling, And roll-ing through the land.

2. I hear the train a-coming,
   a-coming 'round the curve,
   She loosened all her steam and brakes,
   she's straining every nerve. (*Chorus*)

3. The fare is cheap and all can go,
   the rich and poor are there,
   No second class aboard this train,
   no difference in the fare. (*Chorus*)

Go, Tell It on the Mountain

1. When I was a seek-er, I sought both night and day. I asked the Lord to help me, And He showed me the way.

Chorus Go, tell it on the moun-tain, Ov-er the hills and ev-'ry-where. Go, tell it on the moun-tain, Our heav'n-ly Lord__ is born.

2. He made me a watchman
   Upon the city wall.
   And if I serve Him truly,
   I am the least of all. (*Chorus*)

3. In the time of David,
   Some said he was a king.
   And if a child is true born,
   The Lord will hear him sing. (*Chorus*)

He's Got the Whole World in His Hands

1. He's got the whole world_____
2. He's got the wind and rain_____
3. He's got_____ you and me, bro - ther,
4. He's got _____ you and me, sis - ter,

in His hands, He's got the whole world___
in His hands, He's got the wind and rain____
in His hands, He's got___ you and me, bro - ther,
in His hands, He's got___ you and me, sis - ter,

in His hands, He's got the whole world___
in His hands, He's got the wind and rain____
in His hands, He's got___ you and me, bro - ther,
in His hands, He's got___ you and me, sis - ter,

in His hands, He's got the
in His hands, He's got the
in His hands, He's got the
in His hands, He's got the

whole world in His hands,
whole world in His hands,
whole world in His hands,
whole world in His hands,

I'll Fly Away

1. Some bright morn- ing, when this life is ov - er,

I'll fly a - way:

To a land on God's cel- es- tial shore

I'll fly a - way,

Chorus

I'll fly a - way, Oh Lord - y

I'll fly a - way,

When I die, hal - le - lu - jah, by and by I'll fly a - way,

2. When dark shadows of this life are nigh,
   I'll fly away:
   Like a bird, far from these prison walls
   I'll fly away. (*Chorus*)

3. Just a few more weary days and then,
   I'll fly away:
   To a land where joys will never end
   I'll fly away. (*Chorus*)

I'm on My Way

Chorus

I'm on my way_____ and I won't turn back,_____ I'm on my way_____ and I won't turn back, _____ I'm on my way_____ and I won't turn back,_____ I'm on my way, great God, I'm on my way.

Verses

1. I asked my brother to come with me, etc. (*Chorus*)
2. If he won't come, I'll go alone, etc. (*Chorus*)
3. I asked my sister to come with me, etc. (*Chorus*)
4. If she won't come, I'll go alone, etc. (*Chorus*)
5. I'm on my way to Freedom Land, etc. (*Chorus*)

Jacob's Ladder

1. We are climb-ing Ja-cob's lad-der, We are climb-ing Jac-ob's lad-der, We are climb-ing Jac-ob's lad-der Sol-diers of the cross,_____

2. Every round goes higher, higher, etc.
3. Brother, do you love my Jesus? etc.
4. If you love Him, you must serve Him, etc.
5. We are climbing higher, higher, etc.

Joshua Fought
the Battle of Jericho

Refrain

Dm

Josh -ua fought the bat - tle of____ Jer - i - cho,

A 7   Dm

Jer - i - cho,   Jer - i - cho,

Dm

Josh -ua fought the bat - tle of____ Jer - i - cho,

A 7   Dm   *Verse*

and the walls came tum - bling down.   1. You may

Dm

talk a- bout your kings of Gid - e - on,   You may

talk a- bout your men___ of___ Saul, But there's none like good old Josh - ua at the bat - tle of Jer - i - cho.

2. Now the Lord commanded Joshua:
   "I command you, and obey you must;
   You just march straight to those city walls
   And the wall will turn to dust." (*Refrain*)

3. Straight up to the walls of Jericho
   He marched with spear in hand,
   "Go blow that ram's horn," Joshua cried,
   "For the battle is in my hand." (*Refrain*)

4. Then the lamb ram sheep horns began to blow,
   And the trumpets began to sound,
   And Joshua commanded, "Now children, shout!"
   And the walls came tumbling down. (*Refrain*)

Keep Your Lamps Trimmed and Burning

Chorus

Keep your_ lamps trimmed and burn_____-ing, Keep your
lamps trimmed and burn_____-ing, Keep your___
lamps trimmed and burn_____-ing_____ the
time is draw - ing nigh_____.

Verse

1. Chil - dren, don't get wear - y, chil - dren,
2. Sis - ter, don't stop pray - in', Sis - ter,
3. Bro - ther, don't stop sing - in', bro - ther,

don't   get   wear____ -y, chil - dren,
don't   stop   pray____ -in', sis - ter,
don't   stop   sing____ -in', bro - ther,

don't   get   wear____ -y, 'till your
don't   stop   pray____ -in', 'till your
don't   stop   sing____ -in', 'till your

work   is_____ done.
work   is_____ done.
work   is_____ done.

Lonesome Valley

1. Jesus walked_____ this lonesome valley,_____ He had to walk_____ it by Himself, _____ O nobody else___ could walk it for Him, __ He had to walk it by___ Himself.

2. We must walk this lonesome valley,
   we have to walk it by ourselves,
   O nobody else can walk it for us,
   we have to walk it by ourselves.

3. You must go and stand your trial,
   you have to stand it by yourself,
   O nobody else can stand it for you,
   you have to stand it by yourself.

Mary Had a Baby

G

1. Mar - y had a ba - by, my Lord,

G G D 7

Mar - y had a ba - by, my Lord,

G E m

Mar - y had a ba - by, Mar - y had a ba - by,

C G C G

Mar - y had a ba - by, my Lord,

2. Laid him in a manger, my Lord, etc.

3. She named him King Jesus, my Lord, etc.

4. Shepherds came to see Him, my Lords, etc.

Michael, Row the Boat Ashore

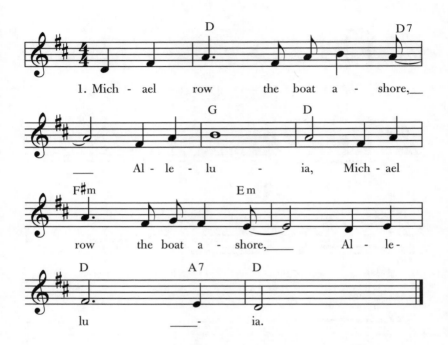

1. Mich - ael row the boat a - shore,___ ___ Al - le - lu - ia, Mich - ael row the boat a - shore,____ Al - le - lu ____ - ia.

2. Michael's boat's a music boat, Alleluia,
   Michael's boat's a music boat, Alleluia.

3. Sister, help to trim the sail, Alleluia,
   Sister, help to trim the sail, Alleluia.

4. Jordan's River is deep and wide, Alleluia,
   Kills the body but not the soul, Alleluia.

5. Jordan's River is deep and wide, Alleluia,
   Meet my mother on the other side, Alleluia.

6. Gabriel, blow the trumpet horn, Alleluia,
   Blow the trumpet loud and long, Alleluia.

Spirituals and Gospel Hymns

Nobody Knows the Trouble I've Seen

No - bo - dy knows the trou-ble I've seen,

No - bo - dy knows but Je - sus.

No - bo - dy knows the trou-ble I've seen,

glo - ry hal - le - lu - jah!

1. Some-times I'm up, some - times I'm down,

oh yes, Lord. Some - times I'm al - most

to the ground, Oh yes, Lord

2. Although you see me going along slow,
   Oh, yes, Lord,
   I have great trials here below,
   Oh, yes, Lord. (*Refrain*)

3. One day when I was walking along,
   Oh, yes, Lord.
   Heaven opened wide, and love came down,
   Oh, yes, Lord. (*Refrain*)

4. Why does old Satan hate me so?
   Oh, yes, Lord,
   He had me once, then let me go,
   Oh, yes, Lord. (*Refrain*)

5. I never will forget the day,
   Oh, yes, Lord,
   When Jesus washed my sins away,
   Oh, yes, Lord. (*Refrain*)

Oh, Won't You Sit Down?

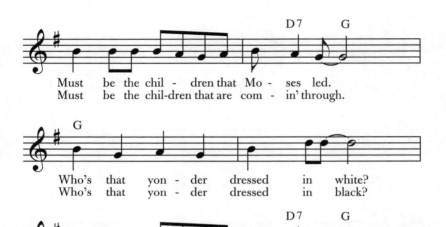

Must   be the chil - dren that Mo - ses led.
Must   be the chil-dren that are com - in' through.

Who's   that   yon - der   dressed   in   white?
Who's   that   yon - der   dressed   in   black?

Must   be the chil-dren of the Is - rael - ite.
Must   be the hyp-o - crites a- turn - in' back.

Old Ark's A-Movin'

Chorus

D

Old ark's a - mov - in',

D

mov - in'; chil - dren, won't you

come a - long? Old ark's a-

A 7   D

mov - in': I Re - joice!

Verse

D

1. How ma-ny days did the wa - ter fall?_____
2. See that sis - ter dressed so fine?_____ She
3. See those child - ren dressed in white?_____ It
4. See those child - ren dressed in red?_____ It

D   A 7 D   (Chorus)

For - ty days and nights and all.
ain't got Je - sus on her mind.
must be the child-ren of the Is - rael - ites.
must be the child-ren that Mo - ses led.

Old Time Religion

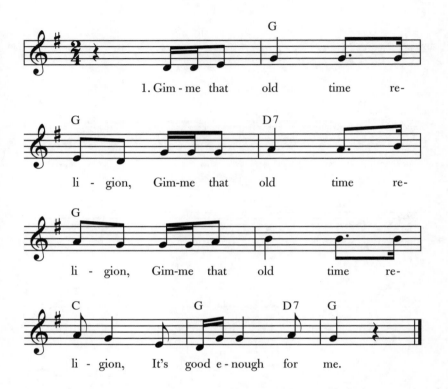

1. Gim - me that old time re-

li - gion, Gim-me that old time re-

li - gion, Gim-me that old time re-

li - gion, It's good e - nough for me.

2. It was good for the Hebrew children, etc.

3. It was good for Paul and Silas, etc.

4. It will take us all to heaven, etc.

One More River

1. Old No - ah built him - self an ark, There's one more ri - ver to cross, And built it all of hick - o - ry bark, There's one more ri - ver to cross.

Chorus
One more ri - ver _____ And that's the ri - ver of Jor - dan;

One more ri - ver _____ There's one more ri - ver to cross. _____

2. The animals came two by two,
   there's one more river to cross,
   The elephant and kangaroo,
   there's one more river to cross. (*Chorus*)

3. The animals came three by three,
   there's one more river to cross,
   The baboon and the chimpanzee,
   there's one more river to cross. (*Chorus*)

4. The animals came four by four,
   there's one more river to cross,
   Old Noah got mad and hollered for more,
   there's one more river to cross. (*Chorus*)

5. The animals came five by five,
   there's one more river to cross,
   The bees came swarming from the hive,
   there's one more river to cross. (*Chorus*)

6. The animals came six by six,
   there's one more river to cross,
   The lion laughed at the monkey's tricks,
   there's one more river to cross. (*Chorus*)

7. When Noah found he had no sail,
   there's one more river to cross,
   He just ran up his old coat tail,
   there's one more river to cross. (*Chorus*)

8. Before the voyage did begin,
   there's one more river to cross,
   Old Noah pulled the gangplank in,
   there's one more river to cross. (*Chorus*)

9. They never knew where they were at,
   there's one more river to cross,
   'Til the old ark bumped on Ararat,
   there's one more river to cross. (*Chorus*)

Rise and Shine

Chorus

Rise___ and shine___, and give God the glo - ry, glo - ry, Rise___ and shine___, and give God the glo - ry, glo - ry, Rise and shine and give God the glo - ry, glo - ry, chil - dren of the Lord._____

Verse

1. The Lord said to No - ah, "There's gon - na be a

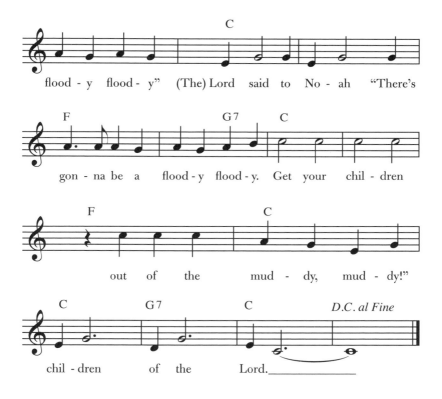

flood - y flood - y" (The) Lord said to No - ah "There's

gon - na be a flood - y flood - y. Get your chil - dren

out of the mud - dy, mud - dy!"

chil - dren of the Lord._____

2. So No-ah, he built him, he built him an ark-y ark-y;
   So No-ah, he built him, he built him an ark-y ark-y;
   Built it out of hick'ry bark-y bark-y,
   Children of the Lord. (*Chorus*)

3. The animals, they came, they came by two-sies, two-sies;
   The animals, they came, they came by two-sies, two-sies;
   Elephants and kang-a-roo-sies, roo-sies,
   Children of the Lord. (*Chorus*)

4. It rained and poured for forty day-sies, day-sies;
   (It) rained and poured for forty day-sies, day-sies;
   Drove those animals nearly cra-zy, cra-zy,
   Children of the Lord. (*Chorus*)

5. The sun came out and dried up the land-y, land-y;
   The sun came out and dried up the land-y, land-y;
   Ev-'ry-one felt fine and dan-dy, dan-dy,
   Children of the Lord. (*Chorus*)

Spirituals and Gospel Hymns

Rock-a-My-Soul

Rock - a - my soul in the bo-som of A - bra - ham;

Rock - a - my soul in the bo-som of A - bra - ham;

Rock - a - my soul in the bo-som of A - bra - ham;

Oh, rock - a my soul. 1. My Lord is
2. His love is

so high, you can't get o - ver Him;
so high, you can't get o - ver it;

so low, you can't get un - der Him;
so low, you can't get un - der it;

so   wide,   you   can't   get   a - round____ Him; You
so   wide,   you   can't   get   a - round____ it; You

must   go   in   at   the   door.
must   go   in   at   the   door.

Somebody's Knockin' at Your Door

Some - bod - y's knock-in' at your door.

knocks like____ Je - sus, *Some - bod - y's*

Knock-in' at your door. O____ sin - ner,

why don't you an - swer? *Some - bod - y's*

knock-in' at your door. Hal - le - lu.

Standin' in the Need of Prayer

broth - er, not my sis - ter, but it's
me, O Lord, Stand- in' in the need of prayer.

2. Not my father, not my mother,
   but it's me, O Lord,
   Standin' in the need of prayer, etc. (*Chorus*)

3. Not my preacher, not my teacher,
   but it's me, O Lord,
   Standin' in the need of prayer, etc. (*Chorus*)

Steal Away

Steal a - way, steal a - way,

Steal a - way, to Je - sus.

Steal a - way, steal a - way home, I

don't have long to stay here.

Verse

1. My Lord_____ calls me, He
2. Green trees are bend - ing, poor
3. My Lord he calls me, He

calls   me   by   the   thun - der;   The
sin - ners   they   stand tremb - ling,   The
calls   me   by   the   light - ning,   The

trum - pet   sounds with - in____   my   soul,   I
trum - pet   sounds with - in____   my   soul,   I
trum - pet   sounds with - in____   my   soul,   I

don't   have   long   to   stay   here.
don't   have   long   to   stay   here.
don't   have   long   to   stay   here.

There's a Little Wheel A-Turning

2. Oh, I feel so very happy in my heart,
   Oh, I feel so very happy in my heart.
   In my heart, in my heart,
   Oh, I feel so very happy in my heart.

This Train

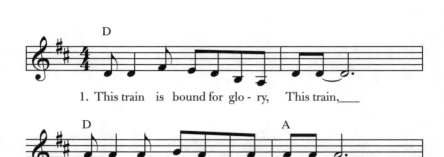

1. This train is bound for glo - ry, This train,___

This train is bound for glo - ry, This train,___

This train is bound for glo - ry

Don't ride noth- in' but the good and ho - ly,

This train is bound for glo - ry, This train!

2. This train don't pull no extras, This train,
   This train don't pull no extras, This train,
   This train don't pull no extras,
   Don't pull nothin' but the midnight special,
   This train don't pull no extras, This train!

Wade in the Water

Leader Sings
All Sing

Chorus

E m

Wade_____ in the wa - ter,_____

E m   A m7   B 7

Wade_____ in the wa - ter, chil - dren,

E m7

Wade_____ in the wa - ter,_____

E m   B 7   E m

God's goin' to trou-ble the wa - ter_____

Verse   E m

1. See that band all dressed in white!__
2. See that band all dressed in red!____

E m   B 7   E m

God's goin' to trou-ble the wa - ter.____ The
God's goin' to trou-ble the wa - ter.____ It

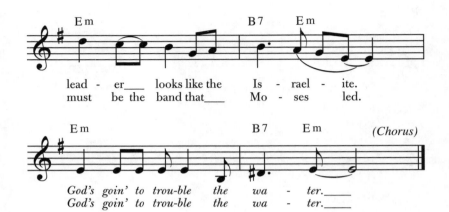

lead - er___ looks like the Is - rael - ite.
must be the band that___ Mo - ses led.

(Chorus)

*God's goin' to trou-ble the wa - ter.*___
*God's goin' to trou-ble the wa - ter.*___

Spirituals and Gospel Hymns

Wayfaring Stranger

1. I'm just a poor way - far - ing strang - er, A - trav - 'ling through this world of woe; But there's no sick - ness, toil nor dan - ger in that bright world to which I go. I'm go - ing there to see my fa - ther,* I'm go - ing there no more to

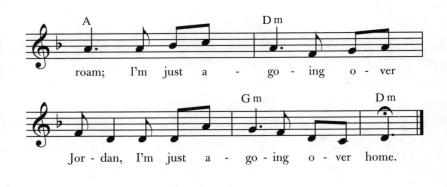

roam; I'm just a - go - ing o - ver

Jor - dan, I'm just a - go - ing o - ver home.

*2. mother   3. sister   4. brother

When the Saints Go Marching In

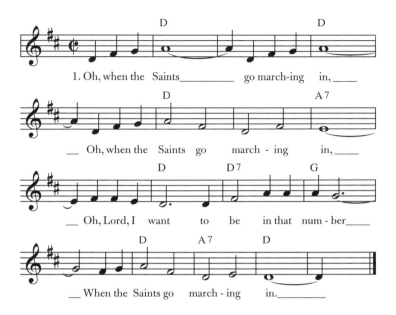

1. Oh, when the Saints _____ go march-ing in, ____
_ Oh, when the Saints go march - ing in, ____
_ Oh, Lord, I want to be in that num - ber ____
_ When the Saints go march - ing in. _____

2. And when the revelation comes,
   And when the revelation comes,
   Oh, Lord, I want to be in that number,
   When the revelation comes.

Continue, as above:
3. Oh, when the new world is revealed . . .
4. Oh, when they gather 'round the throne . . .
5. And when they crown Him King of Kings . . .
6. And when the sun no more will shine . . .
7. And when the moon has turned to blood . . .
8. And when the earth has turned to fire . . .
9. And on that hallelujah day . . .
10. Oh, when the Saints go marching in . . .

American Folk Songs

Baby Bumblebee

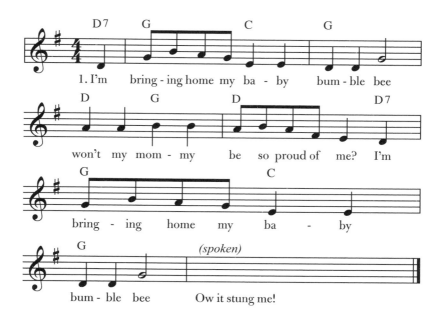

1. I'm bring-ing home my ba-by bum-ble bee won't my mom-my be so proud of me? I'm bring-ing home my ba-by bum-ble bee

(spoken) Ow it stung me!

2. I'm squishing up my baby bumblebee
Won't my mommy be so proud of me
I'm squishing up my baby bumblebee
Won't my mommy be so proud of me
Ew it's sticky!

3. I'm licking up my baby bumblebee
Won't my mommy be so proud of me
I'm licking up my baby bumblebee
Won't my mommy be so proud of me
I don't feel so good.

4. I'm puking up my baby bumblebee
   Won't my mommy be so proud of me
   I'm puking up my baby bumblebee
   Won't my mommy be so proud of me
   What a mess!

5. I'm cleaning up my baby bumblebee
   Won't my mommy be so proud of me
   I'm cleaning up my baby bumblebee
   Won't my mommy be so proud of me
   Mommy are you proud of me?

The Barnyard Song

KENTUCKY MOUNTAINS

1. I had a cat and the cat pleased me, I fed my cat un - der yon - der tree.
2. I had a hen and the hen pleased me, I fed my hen un - der yon - der tree.
3. I had a duck and the duck pleased me, I fed my duck un - der yon - der tree. Duck goes quack, quack, quack, quack,

Hen goes chin - ny - chuck, chin - ny - chuck
Hen goes chin - ny - chuck, chin - ny - chuck

Cat goes fid - dle - i - fee.
Cat goes fid - dle - i - fee.
Cat goes fid - dle - i - fee.

4. I had a goose and the goose pleased me,
   I fed my goose under yonder tree.
   Goose goes swishy, swashy,
   Duck goes quack, quack, quack, quack,
   Cat goes fiddle-i-fee.

5. I had a sheep and the sheep pleased me,
   I fed my sheep under yonder tree.
   Sheep goes baa, baa,
   Goose goes swishy, swashy,
   Cat goes fiddle-i-fee.

6. I had a pig and the pig pleased me,
   I fed my pig under yonder tree.
   Pig goes griffy, gruffy,
   Sheep goes baa, baa,
   Cat goes fiddle-i-fee.

7. I had a cow and the cow pleased me.
   I fed my cow under yonder tree.
   Cow goes moo, moo,
   Pig goes griffy, gruffy,
   Cat goes fiddle-i-fee.

8. I had a horse and the horse pleased me.
   I fed my horse under yonder tree.
   Horse goes neigh, neigh,
   Cow goes moo, moo,
   Cat goes fiddle-i-fee.

With each stanza repeat what the different animals say in the preceding stanza, always ending with "Cat goes fiddle-i-fee."

Bicycle Built for Two

(Daisy Bell)

Harry Dacre

Dai - sy, Dai - sy, give me your an - swer true, I'm half cra - zy all for the love of you. _____ It won't be a sty - lish mar - riage; I can't af - ford a car - riage, _____ But you'll look sweet On the seat of a bi - cy - cle built for two, _____

The Blue Tail Fly
(Jimmy Crack Corn)

Dan Emmett

When I was young I used to wait on

mas - ter and give him his plate, and

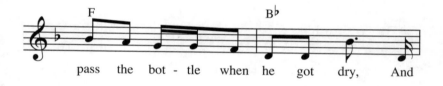

pass the bot - tle when he got dry, And

Brush a - way the blue tail fly.

Jim - my crack corn and I don't care,

American Folk Songs

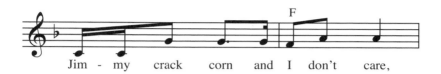

Jim - my crack corn and I don't care,

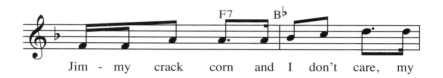

Jim - my crack corn and I don't care, my

mas - ter's gone a - way.

Boom Chick-A-Boom

American Folk Songs

Other Verses:

Barn-yard Style:
I said a moo chicka moo
I said a moo chicka moo
I said a moo chicka bocka chicka bocka chicka moo...

Underwater:
sing with fingers dribbling against your lips
Loud: as loud as you can!
Slowly: as slow and drawn out as possible
Opera: sing in an opera voice
Tongue in Cheek

Valley Girl:
I said, like, boom!
I said, like, boom chicka-boom!
I said, like, booma-chicka, like, rocka-chicka, like, gag me with a spoon!
Like, uh-huh!
Like, for sure!
Like, same thing...

Janitor Style:
I said a Broom-Pusha-Broom,
I said a Broom-Pusha-Broom,
I said a Broom-pusha-mopa-pusha-mopa-pusha-broom

Flower Style:
I said a bloom.
I said a bloom chica bloom.
I said a bloom chica blossom chica blossom chica bloom...

Race Car Style:
I said a vroom.
I said a vroom shifta vroom.
I said a vroom shifta grind-a shifta grind-a shifta vroom...

Astronaut Style:
I said a moon.
I said a shoot-me-to-the-moon.
I said a shoot me blast me shoot me blast me shoot-me-to-the-moon...

Mr. Rogers Style:
Can you say boom?
Can you say boom chica boom?
Can you say boom chica rocka chica rocka chica boom?
Can you say uh-huh?
Can you say oh yeah?
I knew you could!

Bound for the Promised Land

EARLY AMERICAN

1. On_____ Jor - dan's storm_____ - y banks I stand and cast a wish___ - ful eye, To_____ Ca - naan's fair and hap - py land where my pos - ses - sions lie. I am bound for the prom - ised

2. Oh_____ the trans - port_____ - ing rapt' - rous scene that ri - ses to____ my sight. Sweet_____ fields ar___ - rayed in liv - ing green, and__ ri vers__ of de - light.

3. There __ gen - 'rous fruits_____ that nev - er fail on trees im - mor___ - tal grow; There_____ rocks and__ hills and brooks and vales with__ milk and__ hon - ey flow.

4. Soon___ will the Lord_____ my soul pre - pare for joys be - yond___ the skies; Where____ ne - ver___ ceas - ing pleas - ures roll, and__ prais - es___ ne - ver die.

land,_____I'm bound for the prom - ised

land; O_____ who will___ come and

go with me? I am bound for the prom - ised

land.

Buffalo Gals

1. As I was wan - d'ring down the street,

down the street, down the street, a

pret - ty girl I chanced to meet, oh,

she was fair to view.

Refrain

Then Buf - fa - lo gals, will you

come out to - night, will you come out to - night, will you

come out   to - night, Then   Buf - fa - lo   gals, will   you

come out   to - night, And dance by the light of the   moon?

2. I stopped her and I had some talk,
   had some talk, had some talk,
   Her foot covered up the whole sidewalk,
   and left no room for me. (*Refrain*)

3. She's the prettiest gal I've seen in my life,
   seen in my life, seen in my life,
   I wish that she could be my wife,
   Then we would part no more. (*Refrain*)

Cindy

APPALACHIA

1. I wish I had a nick-el, I wish I had a dime, I wish I had a pret-ty girl to love me all the time. *Chorus* Get a-long home, Cin - dy, Cin - dy, Get a-long home, Cin - dy, Cin - dy, Get a-long home, Cin - dy, Cin - dy, I'll mar-ry you some day.

2. You ought to see my Cindy,
   She lives a-way down south,
   And she's so sweet the honey bees,
   Swarm around her mouth. (*Chorus*)

3. The first time I saw Cindy,
   She was standing in the door.
   Her shoes and stockings in her hand,
   Her feet all over the floor. (*Chorus*)

4. She took me to the parlor,
   She cooled me with her fan,
   She said I was the prettiest thing,
   In the shape of mortal man. (*Chorus*)

5. I wish I were an apple,
   A-hanging on a tree,
   And every time my Cindy passed,
   She'd take a bite of me. (*Chorus*)

6. I wish I had a needle,
   As fine as I could sew,
   I'd sew that gal to my coat tail,
   And down the road I'd go. (*Chorus*)

Clementine

1. In a cav - ern, in a can - yon, Ex - ca-
vat - ing for a mine, Dwelt a min - er for - ty
nine - er, And his daugh - ter Clem - en tine.

Chorus

Oh, my dar - ling, Oh, my dar - ling, Oh, my
dar - ling Clem - en - tine! You are lost and gone for -
ev - er. Dread - ful sor - ry, Clem - en - tine!

2. Light she was, and like a fairy,
   And her shoes were number nine,
   Herring boxes without topses,
   Sandals were for Clementine. (*Chorus*)

3. Drove she ducklings to the water
   Every morning just at nine,
   Hit her foot against a splinter,
   fell into the foaming brine. (*Chorus*)

4. Ruby lips above the water
   Blowing bubbles soft and fine;
   As for me, I was no swimmer
   And I lost my Clementine. (*Chorus*)

5. How I missed her, how I missed her,
   How I missed my Clementine.
   Then I kissed her little sister,
   And forgot dear Clementine. (*Chorus*)

Down by the Old Millstream

Down by the old mill stream, Where I first met you, With your eyes so blue, dressed in ging - ham, too. It was there I knew, That you loved me

true. You were six - teen, My vil - lage

Queen, Down by the old mill - stream.

The version of this song that appears below adds opposites to some words in each line. The additional words are sung on the same note as the immediately preceding word—except the final phrase, which is sung very, very slowly to the tune of the equivalent phrase of "How Dry I Am."

> Down by the old (not the new, but the old)
>> millstream (not the river, but the stream),
> Where I first (not last, but first)
>> met you (not me, but you),
> With your eyes (not your ears, but your eyes)
>> so blue (not green, but blue),
> Dressed in gingham (not silk, but gingham)
>> too (not one, but two).
> It was there (not here, but there)
>> I knew (not old, but knew),
> That I loved (not hated, but loved)
>> you true (not false, but true).
> You were sixteen (not fifteen, but sixteen),
> My village queen (not the king, but the queen),
> Down by the old (not the new, but the old)
>> millstream (not the river, but the stream).

Down in the Valley

KENTUCKY

1. Down in the val - ley the val - ley so
2. Ro - ses love sun - shine, vio - lets love

low, Hang your head o - ver, hear the winds
dew, An - gels in hea - ven know I love

blow. Hear the winds blow, dear, hear the winds
you. Know I love you, dear, know I love

blow. Hang your head o - ver, hear the winds blow.
you. An - gels in hea - ven know I love you.

Do Your Ears Hang Low?

2. Do your ears hang low,
    do they waggle to and fro?
    Can you tie them in a knot,
    can you tie them is a bow?
    Can you throw them o'er your shoulder like a continental soldier?
    Do your ears hang low?

3. Do your ears stick out,
    can you waggle them about?
    Can you flap them up and down
    as you fly around the town?
    Can you shut them up for sure when you hear an awful bore?
    Do your ears stick out?

4. Do your ears stand high,
    do they reach up to the sky?
    Do they hang down when they're wet, do they stand up when
    they're dry?
    Can you semaphore your neighbor with the minimum of labor?
    Do your ears stand high?

Erie Canal

I've got a mule, her name is Sal, Fif - teen miles on the E - rie Ca - nal. She's a good old work-er and a good old pal, Fif - teen miles on the E - rie Ca - nal. We've hauled some barg - es in our day, Filled with lumb - er, coal and hay, And we know eve - ry inch of the way from

Al - ba - ny to____ Buf ___ -fa - lo.___

Chorus

Low bridge, eve - ry bod - y down,

Low bridge, 'cause we're

com - ing to a town; And you'll

al - ways know your neigh - bor, You'll

al - ways know your pal, if you've

ev - er na - vi - gat - ed on the

E - rie Ca - nal.

The Glendy Burk

Stephen C. Foster

1. The Glen - dy Burk is a
   I can't stay here for they

migh - ty fast boat, With a might - y fast cap - tain,
work___ too hard, I'm___ bound__ to leave this

too; He sits up there on the
town; I'll take my duds and___

hur - ri - cane roof, And he keeps an eye on the

crew. tote 'em on my back when the

Glen - dy Burk comes down.

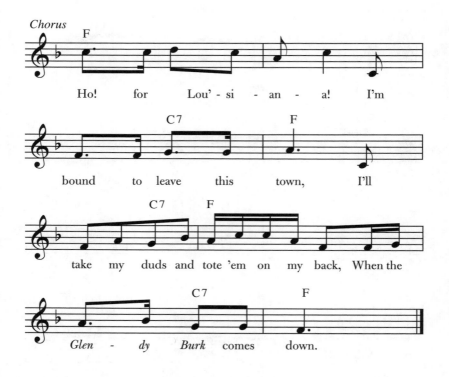

Chorus

Ho! for Lou' - si - an - a! I'm bound to leave this town, I'll take my duds and tote 'em on my back, When the Glen - dy Burk comes down.

2. The *Glendy Burk* has a funny old crew,
   and they sing the boatman's song,
   They burn the pitch and the pine knot, too,
   just to shove the boat along;
   The smoke goes up and the engine roars
   and the wheel goes round and round,
   Then fare you well, for I'll take a little ride
   when the *Glendy Burk* comes down.

Good Night, Ladies

Good night, la-dies, _____ Good night

la-dies _____ Good night, la-dies, _____ We're

going to leave you now. _____

Mer-ri-ly we roll a-long, roll a-long, roll a-long,

Mer-ri-ly we roll a-long, O'er the dark blue sea.

Ham and Eggs

American Folk Songs

Hush, Little Baby

1. Hush lit-tle ba-by, don't say a word

Dad-dy's gon-na buy you a mock-ing bird, And

if that mock-ing bird won't sing,

Dad-dy's gon-na buy you a dia-mond ring, (And)

2. And if that diamond rings turns to brass,
   Daddy's gonna buy you a looking glass,
   And if that looking glass gets broke,
   Daddy's gonna buy you a billy goat.

3. And if that billy goat won't pull,
   Daddy's gonna buy you a cart and bull,
   And if that cart and bull turn over,
   Daddy's gonna buy you a dog named Rover.

4. And if that dog named Rover won't bark,
   Daddy's gonna buy you a horse and cart,
   And if that horse and cart fall down,
   You'll still be the sweetest little baby in town.

I've Been Working on the Railroad
(DINAH)

I've been work - ing on the rail - road

all the live -long day; I've been work - ing on the

rail - road to pass the time a - way.

Don't you hear the whis - tle blow - ing?

Rise up so ear - ly in the morn.

Don't you hear the cap - tain shout - ing,

Din - ah blow your horn.

Di - nah won't you blow,   Di - nah won't you blow.

Di - nah won't you blow your   horn?_____

Di - nah won't you blow,   Di - nah won't you blow.

Di - nah won't you blow your   horn?

Someone's in the kitch-en with   Din - ah,

Someone's in the kitch-en I   know,_____

Someone's in the kitch-en with   Din - ah,

Strum-ming on the old ban - jo.

Fee fie fid - dle - ee - i - o,

Fee fie fid - dle - ee - i - o,

Fee fie fid - dle - ee - i - o,

Strum-ming on the old ban - jo.

Little 'Liza Jane

You got a gal and I got none,
Lit-tle 'Li - za Jane; Come my love and
be my one, Lit-tle 'Li - za Jane.

Chorus

Oh, E - li - za, Lit-tle 'Li - za Jane;

Oh, E - li - za, Lit-tle 'Li - za Jane;

Looby Loo

Here we go loo - by loo, Here we go loo - by light, Here we go loo - by loo, all on a Sat - ur - day night. _____ (1.) I put my right hand in, _____ I put my right hand out, _____ I give my right hand a shake, shake, shake, and turn my-self a - bout. (Oh!)

2. I put my left hand in, etc.
3. I put my right foot in, etc.
4. I put my left foot in, etc.
5. I put my head right in, etc.
6. I put my whole self in, etc.

Mama Don't Allow

2. Mama don't allow no foot stomping round here. (2X)
   But we don't care what Mama don't allow.
   We're gonna stamp our feet anyhow.
   Mama don't allow no foot stomping round here.

Add the following actions:

3. Thigh slapping

4. Head tapping

The Man Who Has Plenty of Good Peanuts

joy - ful,   joy - ful,   joy - ful

Oh,   that will be   joy - ful,   when

his   pea - nuts   are   gone!_____

Mountain Dew

1. Down the road here from me there's an old hol - low tree, Where you lay down a dol - lar or two,_____ If you hush up your mug they will fill up your jug with that good old moun - tain dew.

Chorus

They call it that

good old moun - tain dew, And them that re - fuse it are few. You may go 'round the bend, but you'll come back a - gain for that good old_____ moun - tain___ dew.

2. My uncle Bill has a still on the hill,
   Where he runs off a gallon or two.
   You can tell if you sniff and you get a good whiff
   That he's making that good old mountain dew. (*Chorus*)

3. The preacher came by with a tear in his eye,
   He said that his wife had the flu.
   We told him he ought to give her a quart
   Of that good old mountain dew. (*Chorus*)

4. My brother Mort is sawed off and short,
   He measures just four-foot-two;
   But he thinks he's a giant when they give him a pint
   Of that good old mountain dew. (*Chorus*)

My Bonnie

1. My Bon - nie lies o - ver the o - cean,
2. Oh, blow ye winds o - ver the o - cean,

_____ My Bon - nie lies o - ver the sea, _____
_____ Oh, blow ye winds o - ver the sea, _____

_____ My Bon - nie lies o - ver the o - cean, ___
_____ Oh, blow ye winds o - ver the o - cean, ___

_____ Oh, bring back my Bon - nie to me. _____
_____ And, bring back my Bon - nie to me. _____

Bring back, bring back, Bring back my

Bon - nie to me, to me. me, _____

American Folk Songs

Oh! Susanna

STEPHEN FOSTER

1. I _____ came from Al - a -
2. It _____ rained all night the

ba - ma With my ban - jo on my knee, I'm __
day I left, The weath-er it was dry; The __

goin to Loui - si - an - a My _____ true love for to
sun so hot I froze to death; Su - san - na, don't you

see; Oh, Su - san - na, Oh, don't you cry for
cry.

me, I've _____ come from Al - a -

ba - ma With a ban - jo on my knee.

On Top of Old Smokey

1. On top of old Smo -
2. Oh, court - ing is plea -
3. A thief will just rob

key _____ All cov - ered with
sure _____ And part - ing is
you _____ of all that you

snow, _____ I
grief, _____ But a
save, _____ But a

lost my true lov - er _____ By ___
false heart - ed lov - er _____ is ___
false heart - ed lov - er _____ will ___

court - ing too slow. _____
worse than a thief. _____
lead to the grave. _____

Over the River and Through the Wood

Lydia Maria Childs

O - ver the riv - er and through the wood, To grand - fa - ther's house we go:_____ The horse knows the way to car - ry the sleigh, Through the white and drift - ed snow._____ O - ver the riv - er and through the wood, Oh, how the wind does blow!_____ It

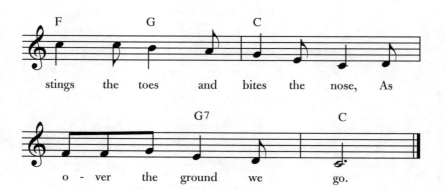

stings the toes and bites the nose, As

o - ver the ground we go.

Polly Wolly Doodle

1. Oh,   I   went   down   South   for   to
2. Oh,   my   Sal   she   is   a_____

see   my   Sal,   Sing - ing   Pol - ly   Wol - ly   Doo - dle   all   the
maid - en   fair,   Sing - ing   Pol - ly   Wol - ly   Doo - dle   all   the

day;   My____   Sal   she   is   a____
day;   With___   curl - y   eyes   and__

spunk - y   gal,   Sing - ing   Pol - ly   Wol - ly   Doo - dle   all   the
laugh - ing   hair,   Sing - ing   Pol - ly   Wol - ly   Doo - dle   all   the

day.   Fare   thee   well,   fare   thee
day.

well,   fare thee well   my   fair - y   fay,   For I'm

goin' to Lou' - si - an - a, For to see my Su - sy - a - na, Sing - ing Pol - ly Wol - ly Doo - dle all the day.

Reuben and Rachel

(Girls) 1. Reu - ben, Reu - ben, I've been think - ing
(Boys) O my good - ness' gra - cious, Ra - chel,

what a grand world this would be,
what a strange world this would be,

If the men were all trans - port - ed
If the men were all trans - port - ed

far be - yond the North - ern Sea.
far be - yond the North - ern Sea.

2. *(Girls)* Reuben, Reuben, I've been thinking
What a fine life girls would lead
If they had no men about them,
None to tease them, none to heed.

(Boys) Rachel, Rachel, I've been thinking
Men would have a merry time
If at once they were transported
Far beyond the salty brine.

The Riddle Song

KENTUCKY

1. I gave my love a cher - ry with -
2. How can there be a cher - ry with -
3. A cher - ry, when it's bloom - ing, it

out a stone; I gave my love a chick-en with -
out a stone? How can there be a chick-en with -
has no stone; A chick-en when it's peep-ing, it

out a bone; I gave my love a ring _____ that
out a bone? How can there be a ring _____ that
has no bone; A ring, when it's a - roll-ing, ____ it

has no end; I
has no end; How
has no end; A

gave my love a ba - by with no cry - in'.
can there be a ba - by with no cry - in'?
ba - by, when it's sleep-ing there's no cry - in'.

She'll Be Comin' 'Round the Mountain

1. She'll be com-in' 'round the moun-tain when she comes,_____ She'll be com-in' 'round the moun-tain when she comes,_____ She'll be com-in' 'round the moun-tain, she'll be com-in' 'round the moun-tain, she'll be

com - in' 'round the moun - tain when she

comes._____

2. She'll be drivin' six white horses when she comes, . .
.
3. Oh, we'll all go out to meet her when she comes, . . .

4. Oh, we'll kill the old red rooster when she comes, . . .

5. And we'll all have chicken dumplings when she comes, . . .

Shoo, Fly

Shoo, fly, don't both - er me, Shoo, fly, don't
both - er me, Shoo, fly, don't both - er me, For
I be - long to some - bo - dy. I feel, I feel, I
feel, I feel like a morn - ing star, I
feel, I feel, I feel, I feel like a morn - ing
star. So, Shoo, fly, don't both - er me

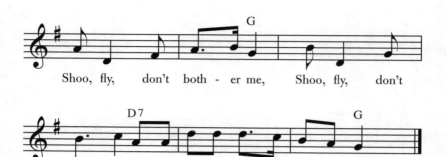

Shoo, fly, don't both - er me, Shoo, fly, don't

both - er me, For I be - long to some-bo - dy.

Skip to My Lou

Flies in the but-ter-milk, Shoo, fly, shoo,

Flies in the but-ter-milk, Shoo, fly, shoo,

Flies in the but-ter-milk, Shoo, fly, shoo,

Skip to my lou, my dar - ling.

Chorus

Lou, lou, Skip to my lou,

Lou, lou, Skip to my lou,

American Folk Songs

Sourwood Mountain

1. Chick - en crow-ing on Sour - wood Moun - tain

Hey de ing dang did - dle al - ly day.

So man - y pret - ty girls I can't count them,

Hey de ing dang did - dle al - ly day.

My true love, she lives in Letch - er,

Hey de ing dang did - dle al - ly day.

She won't come and I won't fetch her,

Hey de ing dang did-dle al-ly day.

2. My true love's a blue-eyed daisy. Hey, etc.
   If I don't get her I'll go crazy, Hey, etc.
   Big dogs bark and little ones bite you, Hey, etc.
   Big girls court and little ones slight you, Hey, etc.

3. My true love lives by the river, Hey, etc.
   A few more jumps and I'll be with her, Hey, etc.
   My true love lives up the hollow, Hey, etc.
   She won't come and I won't follow, Hey, etc.

Tell Me Why

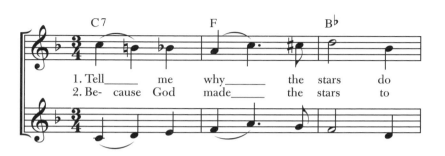

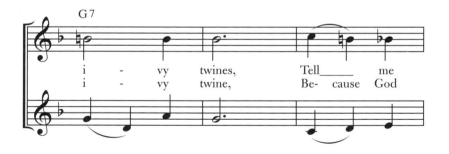

why_____ the sky's so blue, And I will
made_____ the sky so blue, Be- cause God

tell you just why I love you.
made you, that's why I love you.

American Folk Songs

The Titanic

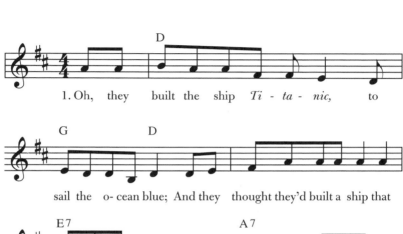

1. Oh, they built the ship *Ti - ta - nic,* to

sail the o- cean blue; And they thought they'd built a ship that

wa - ter would not go through; But the

Lord's al-might-y hand said that ship could ne-ver stand: It was

sad___ when that great___ ship went down. It was

sad, it was sad, it was sad when that great__ ship went

down.   Hus - bands and wives,   lit - tle

chil - dren lost their   lives,   it was

sad___ when that great___ ship went   down.

2. Oh, they sailed from England's shore
   'bout a thousand miles or more;
   And the rich folk,
   they re-fused to 'sociate with the poor;
   So, they put them down below,
   where they'd be the first to go,
   It was sad when the great ship went down. (*Chorus*)

3. Oh, the boat was full of sin, and the sides about to burst,
   When the captain yelled for all the women to go first,
   Oh, the captain tried to wire, but the lines were all on fire.
   It was sad when that great ship went down. (*Chorus*)

4. Oh, they swung the lifeboats out on the deep and raging sea,
   And the entire band struck up with "Nearer My God to Thee."
   All the children wept and cried,
   As the waves swept o'er the side,
   It was sad when the great ship went down. (*Chorus*)

The Water Is Wide

1. The wa - ter is wide, _____ I can-not get
o - ver. And nei - ther
have _____ I wings to __ fly _____. Give me a
boat _____ that can car-ry two _____ and both shall
cross, _____ my true love and I _____

2. I leaned my back against an oak,
Thinking it was a mighty tree,
But first it bent and then it broke,
So did my love prove false to me.

3. I put my hand in some soft bush,
   Thinking the sweetest flower to find,
   I pricked my finger to the bone,
   And left the sweetest flower behind.

4. Oh, love is handsome; love is fine,
   Gay as a jewel when it is new,
   But love grows old and waxes cold,
   And fades away like morning dew.

5. *(Repeat verse 1.)*

Yankee Doodle

1. O fath'r and I went down to camp, a-
long with Cap - tain Good - in', And there we saw the
men and boys as thick as hast - y pud - din'.

Chorus Yan - kee Doo-dle keep it up, Yan - kee Doo-dle
Dan ____ - dy, Mind the mu - sic and the step, And
with the girls be hand - y.

2. And there we saw a thousand men
   As rich as Squire David;
   And what they wasted ev'ry day,
   I wish it could be saved. (*Chorus*)

3. And there was Captain Washington
   Upon a slapping stallion,
   A-giving orders to his men;
   I guess there was a million. (*Chorus*)

4. And then the feathers on his head,
   They looked so very fine, ah!
   I wanted peskily to get
   To give to my Jemima. (*Chorus*)

5. And there I saw a swamping gun,
   Large as a log of maple,
   Upon a mighty little cart;
   A load for father's cattle. (*Chorus*)

Rounds

Are You Sleeping?

(Frere Jacques/Brother John)

4-part Round, prob. French

1. G D G G D G
Are you sleep-ing, are you sleep-ing,
Fre - re Jac - ques, Fre - re Jac - ques,

2. G D G G D G
Bro - ther John, Bro - ther John,
dor - mez - vous, dor - mez - vous,

3.
Mor - ning bells are ring - ing,
Son - nez les ma - ti - nes,

Mor - ning bells are ring - ing,
Son - nez les ma - ti - nes,

4. G D7 G G D7 G
Ding, ding, dong, Ding, ding, dong
din, dan, don, din, dan, don

Dona Nobis Pacem

3-PART ROUND, LATIN

Hey, Ho! Anybody Home?

3-PART ROUND

1. Hey, ho! An-y-bod-y home?

2. Meat or drink nor mon-ey have I none;

3. Still I will be mer_____ - ry.____

Hey, ho! An-y-bod-y home?

I Love the Mountains

5-PART ROUND

1. I love the moun-tains, I love the rol - ling hills,

2. I love the flow - ers, I love the daf - fo-dils,

3. I love the fire__ - side When all the lights are low,

4. Boom-dee-ah-da, boom-dee-ah-da, Boom-dee-ah-da, boom-dee-ah-da,

5. Boom-dee-ah-da, boom-dee-ah-da, Boom-dee-ah-da, boom-dee-ah-da,

Kookaburra

3-PART ROUND, AUSTRALIA, M. SINCLAIR

1. Kook - a - bur - ra sits on an old gum tree, ___

2. Mer - ry, mer - ry king of the bush is he. ___

3. Laugh, kook - a bur - ra, laugh, kook - a - bur - ra

Gay your life must be.

Lovely Evening

3-PART ROUND

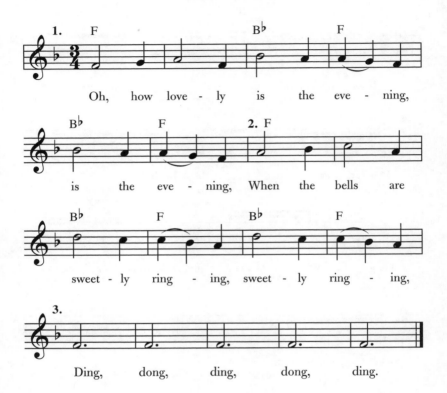

Oh, how love - ly is the eve - ning,

is the eve - ning, When the bells are

sweet - ly ring - ing, sweet - ly ring - ing,

Ding, dong, ding, dong, ding.

Rise Up, O Flame

2-PART ROUND, GERMANY, PRAETORIUS

Rise up, O flame, _____

By _____ thy _____ light glow _____ ing.

Show to us beau _____ - ty, _____

Vi _____ - sion _____ and joy.

Rose, Rose

4-PART ROUND

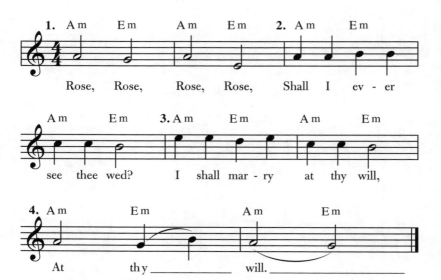

Rose, Rose, Rose, Rose, Shall I ev - er see thee wed? I shall mar - ry at thy will, At thy will. will.

Rounds

Row, Row, Row Your Boat

4-PART ROUND

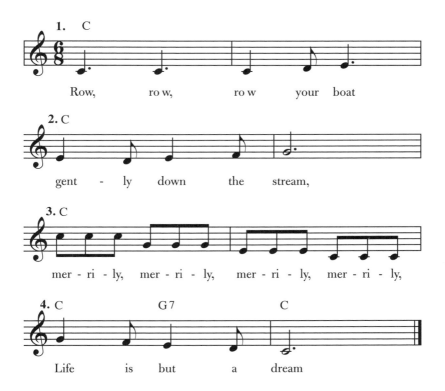

Shalom Chaverim

8-part ROUND, ISRAEL

Sha - lom Cha-ve-rim Sha - lom Cha-ve-rim Sha -

lom Sha - lom L' hit ra __ - ot L'

hit ra __ - ot sha - lom Sha __ - lom.

White Coral Bells

2-PART ROUND, ENGLAND

1. White cor - al bells up -
2. Oh, don't you wish that

on a slen - der stalk, _____
you could hear them ring? _____

Lil - ies of the val - ley deck my
That will hap - pen on - ly when the

gar - den walk. _____
fair - ries sing. _____

Sea Chanteys

Blow the Man Down

Oh, _____ blow the man down, bul - lies,

blow the man down. To me way - aye,

blow the man down! Oh, blow the man

down, bul - lies, blow the man down. Oh,

give me some time to blow the man down.

Blow Ye Winds

'Tis ad - ver - tised in Bos - ton, New York, and Buf - fa - lo, Five hun - dred brave A - mer - i - cans, A - whal - ing for to go ____, sing - ing Blow, ye winds, in the morn - ing, Blow, ye winds, heigh - ho, Haul a - way your run - ning gear, And blow, ye winds, heigh - ho.

Shenandoah
(ACROSS THE WIDE MISSOURI)

1. Oh, Shen - an - doah, I long to hear you, Way, _____ hay, you roll - ing riv - er! Oh, Shen-an-doah, I long to hear you, Way, hay, we're bound a - way, Cross the wide Mis - sour - i.

2. Oh, Shenandoah, I love your daughter,
   Way, hay, you rolling river,
   Oh, Shenandoah, I love your daughter,
   Way, hay, we're bound away,
   'Cross the wide Missouri.

3. Oh, Shenandoah, I love her truly,
   Way, hay, you rolling river,
   Oh, Shenandoah, I love her truly,
   Way, hay, we're bound away,
   'Cross the wide Missouri.

4. I long to see your fertile valley,
   Way, hay, you rolling river,
   I long to see your fertile valley,
   Way, hay, we're bound away,
   'Cross the wide Missouri.

5. Oh, Shenandoah, I'm bound to leave you,
   Way, hay, you rolling river,
   Oh, Shenandoah, I'm bound to leave you,
   Way, hay, we're bound away,
   'Cross the wide Missouri.

Foreign Folk Songs

Alouette

FRENCH CANADA

A - lou - et - te, gen - tille a - lou - et - te

A - lou - et - te, je te plu - me - rai.

Je te plu - me - rai la tete
Je te plu - me - rai le bec

Je te plu - me - rai la tete
Je te plu - me - rai le bec

Et la tete, Et la tete. Oh!

Je te plumerai: (I will pluck your)
1. La tete (head)
2. Le bec (beak)
3. Le nez (nose)
4. Le dos (back)
4. Les pattes (feet)
6. Le cou (neck)

The Ash Grove

WALES

The ash grove, how___ grace - ful, how
Wher - ev - er the___ light through its

plain - ly___ 'tis___ speak - ing, The harp through it___
branch-es___ is___ break - ing, I see the___ kind_

play - ing has lan - guage for me; The__
fa - ces of friends dear to me.

friends of___ my___ child - hood a-

gain are___ be___ - fore me, Each

step brings___ a___ mem - ory as

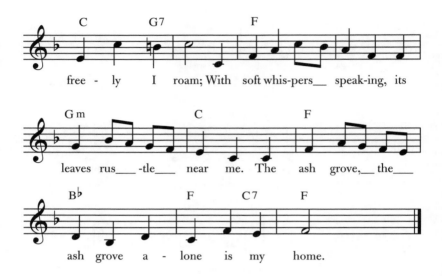

free - ly   I   roam; With soft whis-pers__ speak-ing, its

leaves rus___ -tle___ near me. The   ash grove,__ the___

ash grove a - lone   is   my   home.

Foreign Folk Songs

Au Clair de la Lune

FRANCE

In the eve-ning moon - light,
My good friend Pier - rot, Please give me your
quill pen, Just to write a note.
For my can-dle's out now,
And my fire's out, too; O - pen your front
door, please, May I beg of you!

Au clair de la lune, Mon ami, Pierrot,
Prê-te-moi ta plume, Pour éc-rive un mot.
Ma chandelle est morte, Je n'ai plus de feu;
Ouvre-moi ta porte, Pour l'amour de Dieu!

Auld Lang Syne

ROBERT BURNS, SCOTLAND

1. Should auld ac-quaint-ance be for-got, And nev - er brought to mind? Should auld ac-quaint-ance be for-got, And days of auld lang syne? For auld _____ lang _____ syne, my dear, For auld ___ lang _____ syne; We'll take a cup of kind - ness yet for auld _____ lang _____ syne.

2. We twa ha'e ran aboot the braes,
   And pu'd the gowans fine,
   We're wander'd mony a weary foot
   Sin auld lang syne. (*Chorus*)

3. We twa ha'e sported i' the burn
   Frae mornin' sun till dine,
   But seas between us brain ha'e roared
   Sin auld lang syne. (*Chorus*)

4. And here's a hand, my trusty friend,
   And gie's a hand of thine;
   We'll take a cup of kindness yet
   For auld lang syne. (*Chorus*)

Billy Boy

ENGLAND

1. Oh, _____ where have you been, Bil - ly
Boy, Bil - ly Boy, Oh _____ where have you
been, charm - ing Bil - ly? _____ I have
been to see my wife, she's the joy _____ of my
life, She's a young thing and
can - not leave her moth - er. _____

Foreign Folk Songs

2. Did she bid you to come in, Billy Boy, Billy Boy,
   Did she bid you to come in, charming Billy?
   Yes, she bade me to come in, there's a dimple in her chin,
   She's a young thing and cannot leave her mother.

3. Can she make a cherry pie, Billy Boy, Billy Boy,
   Can she make a cherry pie, charming Billy?
   She can make a cherry pie, quick's a cat can wink her eye,
   She's a young thing and cannot leave her mother.

4. How old is she, Billy Boy, Billy Boy,
   How old is she, charming Billy?
   She's three times six, four times seven,
   twenty-eight and eleven,
   She's a young thing and cannot leave her mother.

The Bridge of Avignon
(SUR LE PONT D'AVIGNON)

FRANCE

Chorus

G   D 7   G

On the bridge (of) A - vi - gnon There is danc - ing,

D 7   G   D 7

there is danc - ing, On the bridge (of) A - vi - gnon

G   D 7   G   *Fine*

there is danc - ing, All a - round.

Verse

D 7   G

1. Gen - tle - men, do like this,

D 7   G   *D.C. al Fine*

then a - gain do like that.

2. Ladies, too do like this, then again do like that.

3. Soldiers, too, do like this, then again do like that.

4. Children, too, do like this, then again do like that.

Chorus
Sur le pont d'Avignon l'on y danse, l'on y danse,

Sur le pont d'Avignon l'on y danse tout en rond.

Verse
1. Les messieurs font comme çi, et puis encore comme ça.

2. Les dames font comme çi, et puis encore comme ça.

3. Les soldats font comme çi, et puis encore comme ça.

4. Les gamins font comme çi, et puis encore comme ça.

The Children's Prayer

ENGELBERT HUMPERDINCK, ENGLAND

When at night I go to sleep, Four - teen an - gels watch do ___ keep; Two my head are guard - ing, Two my feet are guid - ing, Two are on my right hand, Two are on my left hand, Two who warm - ly cov - er, Two who o-er me hov - er, Two to whom 'tis giv - en To light my way to Heav - ___ en.

Foreign Folk Songs

Cielito Lindo
(Beautiful Heaven)

Mexico

Verse

1. From Sier - ra Mo - re - na, Cie - li - to

Lin - do, comes____ soft - ly steal - ing,_____

Laugh-ing eyes,____ black and ro - guish, Cie - li - to

Lin - do, beau - ty re - veal - ing,_____

Chorus

Ay, ay, ay ay!_____

Sing, ban - ish sor - row!_____ To

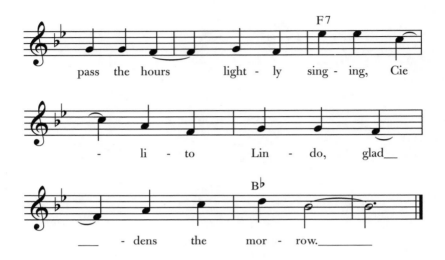

pass the hours light - ly sing - ing, Cie

- li - to Lin - do, glad___

___ - dens the mor - row._____

Verse

2. In the air brightly flashing,
   Cielito Lindo, flies Cupid's feather,
   My heart it is striking,
   Cielito Lindo, wounding forever.

Verse

1. De la Siera Morena, Cielito Lindo, vienen bajando;
   Un parde ojitos negros, Cielito Lindo, de contrabando.

   Chorus: ¡Ay, ay, ay, ay! Canta y no llores,
   Porque cantando se alegran, Cielito Lindo
   los corazones.

Verse

2. Una flecha en aire, Cielito Lindo, lanzo Cupido.
   Y como fue jugando, Cielito Lindo, yo fui el herido.

Cockles and Mussels

IRELAND

1. In Dub - lin's fair cit - y, where girls are so pret - ty, I first set my eyes on sweet Mol - ly Ma - lone, As she wheeled her wheel bar-row through streets broad and nar-row, Cry -ing "Cock-les and mus-sels, A- live, a - live oh!" A - live, a - live

oh!_____ A - live, a - live oh!_____ Cry - ing

"Cock - les and mus - sels, a - live, a - live, oh!"

2. She was a fishmonger, but sure, 'twas no wonder,
   For so were her father and mother before;
   And they wheeled their wheelbarrow
   through streets broad and narrow,
   Crying "Cockles and mussels, alive, alive oh!"
   (Refrain)

3. She died of a fever and no one could save her,
   And that was the end of sweet Molly Malone;
   Now her ghost wheels her barrow
   through streets broad and narrow,
   Crying "Cockles and mussels, alive, alive oh!"
   (Refrain)

Frog Went A-Courting

ENGLAND

1. A frog went a-court-ing and he did ride, uh, huh!_____ A frog went a-court-ing and he did ride, uh, huh!_____ A frog went a-courting and he did ride, a sword and pis-tol by his side, uh, huh!_____

2. He rode right to Miss Mousie's door, uh, huh!
   He rode right to Miss Mousie's door, uh, huh!
   He rode right to Miss Mousie's door
   Where he had often gone before, uh, huh!

3. He took Miss Mousie on his knee,
   Said, "Miss Mousie, will you marry me?" uh, huh!, etc.

4. "Without my Uncle Rat's consent
   I couldn't marry the president!" uh, huh!, etc.

5. Uncle Rat gave his consent,
   So they got married and off they went, uh, huh!, etc.

6. Now, where will the wedding supper be?
   Away down yonder by the hollow tree, uh, huh!, etc.

7. Who's going to make the wedding gown?
   Old Miss Toad from the lily pond, uh, huh!, etc.

8. Now, what will the wedding supper be?
   Two big green peas and a black-eyed pea, uh, huh! etc.

9. Now, the first to come was a big white moth,
   She spread down a white table cloth, uh, huh! etc.

10. If you want this song again to ring,
    Make it up yourself and start to sing, uh, huh! etc.

Greensleeves

(WHAT CHILD IS THIS)

ENGLAND

1. A - las, my love,___ you do me wrong,___ To

cast me off___ dis - court - eous - ly And

I have loved___ you for so long,___ De -

light - ing in___ your com - pan - y.

Refrain

Green - sleeves___ was all my joy,___

Green___ - sleeves___ was my de - light

Green - sleeves was my heart of gold,____ and

who but my lad_____-y Green - sleeves.

2. I long have waited at your hand
   To do your bidding as your slave,
   And waged, have I, both life and land
   Your love and affection for to have. (*Refrain*)

3. If you intend thus to disdain
   It does the more enrapture me,
   And even so, I will remain
   Your lover in captivity. (*Refrain*)

4. Alas, my love, that yours should be
   A heart of faithless vanity,
   So here I meditate alone
   Upon your insincerity. (*Refrain*)

5. Ah, Greensleeves, now farewell, adieu,
   To God I pray to prosper thee,
   For I remain thy lover true,
   Come once again and be with me. (*Refrain*)

Kumbayah

AFRICA

Chorus

Kum - ba - yah, my Lord,_____

Kum - ba - yah,_____

Kum - ba - yah, my Lord,_____

Kum - ba - yah,_____

Kum - ba - yah, my Lord,_____

Kum - ba - yah,_____

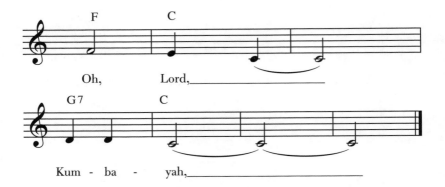

Oh, Lord,_____

Kum - ba - yah,_____

1. Someone's singing, Lord, kumbayah, etc. (*Chorus*)

2. Someone's weeping, Lord, kumbayah, etc. (*Chorus*)

3. Someone's dancing, Lord, kumbayah, etc. (*Chorus*)

4. Someone's praying, Lord, kumbayah, etc. (*Chorus*)

Lavender's Blue

ENGLAND

1. Lav - en - der's blue, dil - ly, dil - ly,

lav - en - der's green,

When I am king, dil - ly, dil - ly,

you shall be queen.

Who told you so, dil - ly, dil - ly, who told you so?

'Twas mine own heart, dil - ly, dil - ly, that told me so.

Loch Lomond

SCOTLAND

1. By___ yon bon-nie banks and by yon bon-nie braes where the
sun shines bright on Loch Lo - mond, Where
me and my true love were ev - er wont to gae, On the
bon - nie, bon - nie banks of Loch Lo - mond. Oh!
ye'll take the high road, and I'll take the low road And
I'll be in Scot - land a - fore ye, But

me   and my true   love we'll   nev - er meet a - gain,   On the

bon - nie, bon - nie banks   of   Loch   Lo - mond.

2. 'Twas there that we parted in yon shady glen
   On the steep, steep side of Ben Lomond,
   Where in purple hue the highland hills we view,
   And the moon coming out in the gloaming.

   (Refrain)

3. The wee birdies sing, and the wild flowers spring,
   And in sunshine the waters are sleeping.
   But the broken hearts kens nae second spring again,
   Though the waeful may cease frae their greeting.

   (Refrain)

Lullaby

JOHANNES BRAHMS, GERMANY

1. Lul - la - by and good - night with _____ ro - ses be - dight, _____ with _____ down o - ver _____ spread is _____ ba - by's wee bed; Lay thee down now and rest, May thy slum - bers be blest, Lay thee down now and rest, May thy slum - bers be blest.

2. Lullaby and goodnight, thy mother's delight,
   Bright angels beside my darling abide.
   They will guard thee at rest, thou shalt wake on my breast,
   They will guard thee at rest, thou shalt wake on my breast.

1. Guten Abend, gut' Nacht, mit Rosen bedacht,
   Mit Naglein besteckt, schlupf unter die Deck.
   Morgen fruh, wenn Gott will wirst du weider geweckt;
   Morgen fruh, wenn Gott will wirst du weider geweckt.

Mary Ann

CARIBBEAN/CALYPSO

All night, all day, Miss Ma-ry Ann,

Down by the sea - side sift-ing sand.

Ev - ery - bod-y down there join the band,

Down by the sea - side sift-ing sand.

Verse

If you come to our Port of Spain, you'll

nev - er want to go home a - gain

You'll do ev - er - y - thing you can,

Just to be round Miss Ma - ry Ann.

The More We Get Together

GERMANY

The more we get to - geth - er, to -
geth - er, to - geth - er, The more we get to -
geth - er, the hap - pier we'll be! For
your friends are my friends, and my friends are
your friends. The more we get to -
geth - er, the hap - pier we'll be!

Foreign Folk Songs

Paper of Pins

BRITISH ISLES

(Boys) I'll give to you a
(Girls) I'll not ac - cept your

pa - per of pins, And that's the way true
pa - per of pins, If that's the way your

love be - gins, if you will mar - ry
love be - gins, And I'll not mar - ry

me, me, me, If you will mar - ry me.
you, you, you, And I'll not mar - ry you.

2. I'll give to you a satin gown with silken
      tassels all around,
   If you will marry me, me, me, if you will marry me.
   I'll not accept your satin gown with silken
      tassels all around,
   And I'll not marry you, you, you, and I'll not marry you.

3. I'll give to you a dress of red all sewn
      around with golden thread
   If you will marry me, me, me, if you will marry me.
   I'll not accept your dress of red all sewn
      around with golden thread
   And I'll not marry you, you, you, and I'll not marry you.

4. I'll give to you my big black horse that's paced
      the meadow all across.
   If you will marry me, me, me, if you will marry me.
   I'll not accept your big black horse that's paced
      the meadow all across,
   And I'll not marry you, you, you, and I'll not marry you.

5. I'll give to you my hand and heart that you
      and I may never part,
   If you will marry me, me, me, if you will marry me.
   I'll not accept your hand and heart that you
      and I may never part,
   And I'll not marry you, you, you, and I'll not marry you.

6. I'll give to you a house and land, a William goat,
   A hired hand,
   If you will marry me, me, me, if you will marry me.
   I'll not accept your house and land, your William goat,
   your hired hand,
   And I'll not marry you, you, you, and I'll not marry you.

7. I'll give to you the key to my chest with gold
   whenever you request,
   If you will marry me, me, me, if you will marry me.
   I'll not accept the key to your chest with gold
   whenever I request,
   And I'll not marry you, you, you, and I'll not marry you.

8. O, now I see that money is king and your life
   didn't mean a thing.
   So I won't marry you, you, you, so I won't marry you.
   And old maid, then, I'll have to be, another I won't
   wed, you see,
   So won't you marry me, me, me, so won't you
   marry me?

Pop! Goes the Weasel

ENGLAND

1. All a - round the cob - bler's bench

Mon - key chased the wea - sel,

Mon - key thought 'twas all in fun,

Pop! goes the wea - sel.

Pen - ny for a spool___ of thread,

Pen - ny for a nee - dle,

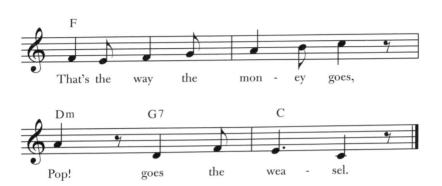

That's the way the mon - ey goes,

Pop! goes the wea - sel.

2. The painter needs a ladder and brush,
   the artist needs an easel,
   The dancers need a fiddler's tune,
   Pop! goes the weasel;
   I've no time to wait or to sigh,
   or to tell the reason why,
   Kiss me quick, I'm off, good-by,
   Pop! goes the weasel.

Sarasponda

Poss. Holland (Spinning Song)

Foreign Folk Songs

Scarborough Fair

Englend

1. Are you go - ing to Scar - bor-ough Fair? _____ Pars - ley

sage, rose - mar - y and thyme; _____ Re -

mem - ber me to one that lives there, _____ For

she was once a true love of mine._____

2. Tell her to make me a cambric shirt.
   Parsley, sage, rosemary and thyme;
   Without a seam or fine needle work,
   And then she'll be a true love of mine.

3. Tell her to wash it in yonder dry well,
   Parsley, sage, rosemary and thyme;
   Where water ne'er sprung, nor drop of rain fell,
   And then she'll be a true love of mine.

4. Tell her to dry it on yonder thorn,
   Parsley, sage, rosemary and thyme;
   Which never bore blossom since Adam was born,
   And then she'll be a true love of mine.

5. Tell him to find me an acre of land,
   Parsley, sage, rosemary and thyme;
   Between the sea foam and the sea sand,
   Or never be a true love of mine.

6. Tell him to plough it with a lamb horn,
   Parsley, sage, rosemary and thyme;
   And sow it all over with one peppercorn,
   Or never be a true love of mine.

7. Tell him to reap it with a sickle of leather,
   Parsley, sage, rosemary and thyme;
   And tie it all up with a peacock's feather,
   Or never be a true love of mine.

8. When he has done and finished his work,
   Parsley, sage, rosemary and thyme;
   Then come to me for his cambric shirt,
   And he shall be a true love of mine.

This Old Man

ENGLAND

1. This old man, he played one, He played nick - nack on my thumb, With a nick - nack pad-dy whack give the dog a bone! This old man came roll - ing home.

2. This old man, he played two,
   He played nick-nack on my shoe.

3. This old man, he played three,
   He played nick-nack on my knee.

4. This old man, he played four,
   He played nick-nack on my door.

Foreign Folk Songs   191

5. This old man, he played five,
   He played nick-nack on my hive.

6. This old man, he played six,
   He played nick-nack on my sticks.

7. This old man, he played sev'n,
   He played nick-nack till elev'n.

8. This old man, he played eight,
   He played nick-nack on my gate.

9. This old man, he played nine,
   He played nick-nack on my spine.

10. This old man, he played ten,
    He played nick-nack over again.

Vesper Hymn

RUSSIA

1. Hark! the ves - per hymn is steal - ing,
o-er the wa - ters soft and clear; Near - er yet and
near - er peal - ing, soft it breaks up - on the ear
Ju - bi - la - te! Ju - bi - la - te! Ju - bi - la - te!
A__ - men. Far - ther now and far - ther steal - ing,
soft it fades up ___ - on the ear.

2. Now like moonlight waves retreating, to the
      shore it dies along;
   Now like angry surges meeting, breaks the
      mingled tide of song.
   Jubilate! Jubilate! Jubilate! Amen;
   Jubilate! Jubilate! Jubilate! Amen.
   Hark! Again like waves retreating, to the shore
      it dies along.

3. Once again sweet voices ringing, louder still
      the music swells;
   While on summer breezes winging, comes the
      chime of vesper bells.
   Jubilate! Jubilate! Jubilate! Amen;
   Jubilate! Jubilate! Jubilate! Amen.
   On the summer breezes winging, fades the chime
      of vesper bells.

We Gather Together

ENGLISH WORDS BY THEODORE BAKER, HOLLAND

1. We gath - er to - geth - er to ask the Lord's bless - ing; He chas - tens and has - tens His will to make known. The wick - ed op - press - ing, now cease from dis - tress - ing. Sing prais - es to His name; He for - gets not His own.

2. Beside us to guide us, our God with us joining,
   Ordaining, maintaining His kingdom divine.
   So from the beginning, the fight we were winning.
   Thou, Lord, wast at our side;
   All glory be thine.

3. We all do extol Thee, Thou leader triumphant,
   And pray that Thou still our defender wilt be.
   Let Thy congregation escape tribulation.
   Thy name be ever praised!
   O Lord, make us free!

Where Has My LIttle Dog Gone?
(Der Deitcher's Dog)

Septimus Winner, Germany

Oh where, oh where has my lit - tle dog gone? Oh where, oh where can he be? _____ With his ears cut short and his tail cut long, oh where, oh where can he be? _____

Zum Gali Gali

ISRAEL

Chorus

Zum ga - li, ga - li, ga - li, Zum ga - li, ga - li

Verse

1. Pi - o - neers must work ev - 'ry day,
2. Pi - o - neers will sing and ____ dance,
3. Pi - o - neers will work for ____ peace,

From ____ dawn 'til day is ____ done;
Dance the ho - ra in a ____ ring;
From ____ dawn 'til day is ____ done;

From ____ dawn 'til day is ____ done;
Dance the ho - ra in a ____ ring;
From ____ dawn 'til day is ____ done;

There is work for ev - 'ry ____ - one.
With their best gifts, dance and ____ sing.
True ____ peace for ev - 'ry ____ - one.

Hebrew Transliteration:

He-kha-lutz le-maan a-v-dah;

A-vo-dah le-maan he-kha-lutz.

A-vo-dah le-maan he-kha-lutz;

He-kha-lutz le-maan a-vo-dah.

Patriotic Songs

America

Samuel Francis Smith, Henry Carey

1. My coun - try, 'tis of Thee,

Sweet land of li - ber - ty,

Of Thee I sing. Land where my

fa - thers died, Land of the Pil - grim's pride

From ev___ - 'ry___ moun - tain - side

Let___ free - dom ring.

Patriotic Songs

2. My native country, Thee,
    land of the noble free, Thy name I love.
    I love Thy rocks and hills, thy woods and templed hills,
    My heart with rapture thrills Like that above.

3. Let music swell the breeze,
    and ring from all the trees, Sweet freedom's song.
    Let mortal tongues awake, let all that breathe partake,
    Let rocks their silence break, The sound prolong.

4. Our fathers' God, to Thee,
    Author of liberty, To Thee we sing.
    Long may our land be bright with freedom's holy light,
    Protect us by Thy might, Great God, our King!

America the Beautiful

KATHARINE LEE BATES, SAMUEL A. WARD

1. O beau - ti - ful for spa - cious skies, for am - ber waves of grain, For pur - ple moun - tains ma - jes - ties A - bove the fruit - ed plain! A - mer - i - ca! A - mer - i - ca! God shed His grace on thee, and crown thy good with bro - ther - hood From sea to shin - ing sea!

Patriotic Songs

2. O beautiful for Pilgrim feet,
   Whose stern impassioned stress
   A thoroughfare for freedom beat
   Across the wilderness.
   America! America! God mend thine every flaw,
   Confirm thy soul in self-control,
   Thy liberty in law.

3. O beautiful for heroes proved
   In liberating strife,
   Who more than self their country loved,
   And mercy more than life.
   America! America! May God thy gold refine
   Till all success be nobleness
   And every gain divine.

4. O beautiful for patriot dream
   That sees beyond the years,
   Thine alabaster cities gleam
   Undimmed by human tears.
   America! America! God shed His grace on thee,
   And crown thy good with brotherhood
   From sea to shining sea.

Battle Hymn of the Republic

JULIA WARD HOWE, WILLIAM STEFFE

Patriotic Songs

on.   Glo - ry, Glo - ry, hal - le-
lu - jah! Glo - ry, Glo - ry, hal - le-
lu - jah! Glo - ry, Glo - ry, hal - le- lu - jah! His
truth   is   march - ing on.

2. He has sounded forth the trumpet
   that shall never call retreat;
   He is sifting out the hearts of men
   before the judgment seat.
   Oh, be swift, my soul, to answer Him!
   Be jubilant, my feet!
   Our God is marching on. (*Refrain*)

God of Our Fathers

GEORGE W. WARREN, D. C. ROBERTS

1. God of our fa - thers, whose al - might - y hand Leads forth in beau - ty all the star - ry band. Of shin - ing worlds in splen - dor through the skies, Our grate - ful songs be - for Thy throne a - rise.

2. Thy love divine hath led us in the past,
   In this free land by Thee our lot is cast;
   Be Thou our Ruler, Guardian, Guide and Stay,
   Thy word our law, Thy paths our chosen way.

3. Refresh Thy people on their toilsome way,
   Lead us from night to never-ending day;
   Fill all our lives with love and grace divine,
   And glory, laud, and praise be ever Thine.

How Can I Keep from Singing?

Civil War Song

1. My life flows on in
2. Through all the tu - mult
3. What, though the tem - pest

end - less song, ___ a - bove earth's lam - en-
and the strife, ___ I hear the mu - sic
round me 'rears, ___ I know the truth, it

ta - tion, ___ I hear the real though
ring-ing; ___ It sounds and ech - oes
liv - eth. ___ What, though the dark - ness

far off hymn that hails a new cre-
in my soul; How can I keep from
'round me close, songs in the nights it

a - tion. ___ No storm can shake my
singing? ___ No storm can shake my
giv - eth. ___ No storm can shake my

Dm
B♭
in - most calm, while to that Rock I'm
in - most calm, while to that Rock I'm
in - most calm, while to that Rock I'm
F
F
cling - ing It sounds an ech - o
cling - ing Since love is lord of
cling - ing Since love is lord of
B♭
F
F
C7
in my soul, How can I keep from
Heaven and earth, How can I keep from
Heaven and earth, How can I keep from
F
sing - ing?
sing - ing?
sing - ing?

About the Editors

Irene Maddox was associated with music in almost every way possible—she sang, taught music in public schools, was a church accompanist, played professionally in orchestras and Broadway shows; she performed as a soloist in the United States and Europe in front of symphony orchestras, as part of chamber groups, and as part of a flute-guitar duo. She taught flute in her Charlotte, North Carolina, studio, as well as on the staff of the University of North Carolina at Charlotte and Queens College. She performed with organist Mark Andersen as the Andersen-Maddox Duo, who recorded exclusively for International Artists (United States) and Philips (Europe).

A native of Texas and a graduate of North Texas State University, where she received both her BA and MME degrees, Mrs. Maddox studied in Europe with internationally acclaimed flutist Jean-Pierre Rampal. She was founder of the Charlotte Flute Association and an officer of the National Flute Association. Two daughters, Robirene and Melisande, and husband Robert Maddox, a musician/conductor, make up her family.

Equally at ease singing songs such as those in this book or performing as a soloist before 90,000 people, Mrs. Maddox radiated enthusiasm for music.

Rosalyn Cobb worked with both children and adults in many different aspects of music. She concentrated her efforts in Orff-Music and developed many programs in this area for children, senior citizens, and persons with disabilities. She taught at The Community School of the Arts, in Charlotte, North Carolina.

Ms. Cobb completed her studies in organ and piano at Salem College in Winston-Salem, North Carolina, and at The Oberlin Conservatory of Music in Cleveland, Ohio. She appeared as a piano soloist with The Charlotte Symphony Orchestra and toured extensively as accompanist of The Charlotte Choirboys.

Teaching summer classes for gifted children in musical theater, directing church choirs, and maintaining a large private studio of piano students enabled Rosalyn to share with others her enthusiasm for music. Some of her fondest childhood memories were of singing and playing the campfire songs in this book during summer vacations at various camps in the Carolinas.

More books to enjoy around the campfire:

Campfire Stories,
second edition,
by William W. Forgey,
illustrated by Paul G. Hoffman

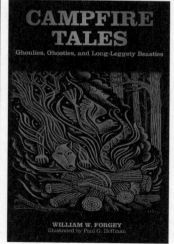

Campfire Tales,
second edition,
by William W. Forgey,
illustrated by Paul G. Hoffman